Francis Frith's
AROUND PENZANCE

PHOTOGRAPHIC MEMORIES

Francis Frith's
AROUND PENZANCE

◆

Des Hannigan

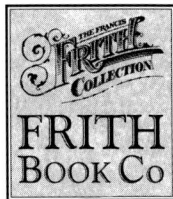

FRITH
BOOK Co

First published in the United Kingdom in 1999 by
Frith Book Company Ltd

Hardback Edition 1999
ISBN 1-85937-069-1

Paperback Edition 2002
ISBN 1-85937-488-3

Reprinted in hardback 2002

British Library Cataloguing in Publication Data

Francis Frith's Around Penzance
Des Hannigan

Frith Book Company Ltd
Frith's Barn, Teffont,
Salisbury, Wiltshire SP3 5QP
Tel: +44 (0) 1722 716 376
Email: info@francisfrith.co.uk
www.francisfrith.co.uk

Printed and bound in Great Britain

AS WITH ANY HISTORICAL DATABASE THE FRITH ARCHIVE IS CONSTANTLY BEING CORRECTED AND IMPROVED
AND THE PUBLISHERS WOULD WELCOME INFORMATION ON OMISSIONS OR INACCURACIES

CONTENTS

FRANCIS FRITH: *Victorian Pioneer*

FRANCIS FRITH, Victorian founder of the world-famous photographic archive, was a complex and multitudinous man. A devout Quaker and a highly successful Victorian businessman, he was both philosophic by nature and pioneering in outlook.

By 1855 Francis Frith had already established a wholesale grocery business in Liverpool, and sold it for the astonishing sum of £200,000, which is the equivalent today of over £15,000,000. Now a multi-millionaire, he was able to indulge his passion for travel. As a child he had pored over travel books written by early explorers, and his fancy and imagination had been stirred by family holidays to the sublime mountain regions of Wales and Scotland. 'What a land of spirit-stirring and enriching scenes and places!' he had written. He was to return to these scenes of grandeur in later years to 'recapture the thousands of vivid and tender memories', but with a different purpose. Now in his thirties, and captivated by the new science of photography, Frith set out on a series of pioneering journeys to the Nile regions that occupied him from 1856 until 1860.

INTRIGUE AND ADVENTURE

He took with him on his travels a specially-designed wicker carriage that acted as both dark-room and sleeping chamber. These far-flung journeys were packed with intrigue and adventure. In his life story, written when he was sixty-three, Frith tells of being held captive by bandits, and of fighting 'an awful midnight battle to the very point of surrender with a deadly pack of hungry, wild dogs'. Sporting flowing Arab costume, Frith arrived at Akaba by camel seventy years before Lawrence, where he encountered 'desert princes and rival sheikhs, blazing with jewel-hilted swords'.

During these extraordinary adventures he was assiduously exploring the desert regions bordering the Nile and patiently recording the antiquities and peoples with his camera. He was the first photographer to venture beyond the sixth cataract. Africa was still the mysterious 'Dark Continent', and Stanley and Livingstone's historic meeting was a decade into the future. The conditions for picture taking confound belief. He laboured for hours in his wicker dark-room in the sweltering heat of the desert, while the volatile chemicals fizzed dangerously in their trays. Often he was forced to work in remote tombs and caves

where conditions were cooler. Back in London he exhibited his photographs and was 'rapturously cheered' by members of the Royal Society. His reputation as a photographer was made overnight. An eminent modern historian has likened their impact on the population of the time to that on our own generation of the first photographs taken on the surface of the moon.

VENTURE OF A LIFE-TIME

Characteristically, Frith quickly spotted the opportunity to create a new business as a specialist publisher of photographs. He lived in an era of immense and sometimes violent change. For the poor in the early part of Victoria's reign work was a drudge and the hours long, and people had precious little free time to enjoy themselves.

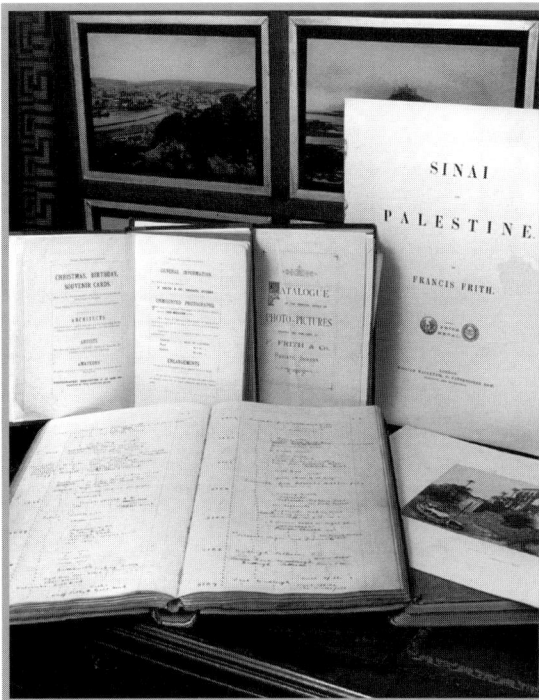

Most had no transport other than a cart or gig at their disposal, and had not travelled far beyond the boundaries of their own town or village. However, by the 1870s, the railways had threaded their way across the country, and Bank Holidays and half-day Saturdays had been made obligatory by Act of Parliament. All of a sudden the ordinary working man and his family were able to enjoy days out and see a little more of the world.

With characteristic business acumen, Francis Frith foresaw that these new tourists would enjoy having souvenirs to commemorate their days out. In 1860 he married Mary Ann Rosling and set out with the intention of photographing every city, town and village in Britain. For the next thirty years he travelled the country by train and by pony and trap, producing fine photographs of seaside resorts and beauty spots that were keenly bought by millions of Victorians. These prints were painstakingly pasted into family albums and pored over during the dark nights of winter, rekindling precious memories of summer excursions.

THE RISE OF FRITH & CO

Frith's studio was soon supplying retail shops all over the country. To meet the demand he gathered about him a small team of photographers, and published the work of independent artist-photographers of the calibre of Roger Fenton and Francis Bedford. In order to gain some understanding of the scale of Frith's business one only has to look at the catalogue issued by Frith & Co in 1886: it runs to some 670

pages, listing not only many thousands of views of the British Isles but also many photographs of most European countries, and China, Japan, the USA and Canada – note the sample page shown above from the hand-written *Frith & Co* ledgers detailing pictures taken. By 1890 Frith had created the greatest specialist photographic publishing company in the world, with over 2,000 outlets – more than the combined number that Boots and WH Smith have today! The picture on the right shows the *Frith & Co* display board at Ingleton in the Yorkshire Dales. Beautifully constructed with mahogany frame and gilt inserts, it could display up to a dozen local scenes.

POSTCARD BONANZA

◆

The ever-popular holiday postcard we know today took many years to develop. In 1870 the Post Office issued the first plain cards, with a pre-printed stamp on one face. In 1894 they allowed other publishers' cards to be sent through the mail with an attached adhesive halfpenny stamp. Demand grew rapidly, and in 1895 a new size of postcard was permitted called the

court card, but there was little room for illustration. In 1899, a year after Frith's death, a new card measuring 5.5 x 3.5 inches became the standard format, but it was not until 1902 that the divided back came into being, with address and message on one face and a full-size illustration on the other. *Frith & Co* were in the vanguard of postcard development, and Frith's sons Eustace and Cyril continued their father's monumental task, expanding the number of views offered to the public and recording more and more places in Britain, as the coasts and countryside were opened up to mass travel.

Francis Frith died in 1898 at his villa in Cannes, his great project still growing. The archive he created continued in business for another seventy years. By 1970 it contained over a third of a million pictures of 7,000 cities, towns and villages. The massive photographic record Frith has left to us stands as a living monument to a special and very remarkable man.

Frith's Archive: *A Unique Legacy*

FRANCIS FRITH'S legacy to us today is of immense significance and value, for the magnificent archive of evocative photographs he created provides a unique record of change in 7,000 cities, towns and villages throughout Britain over a century and more. Frith and his fellow studio photographers revisited locations many times down the years to update their views, compiling for us an enthralling and colourful pageant of British life and character.

We tend to think of Frith's sepia views of Britain as nostalgic, for most of us use them to conjure up memories of places in our own lives with which we have family associations. It often makes us forget that to Francis Frith they were records of daily life as it was actually being lived in the cities, towns and villages of his day. The Victorian age was one of great and often bewildering change for ordinary people, and though the pictures evoke an impression of slower times, life was as busy and hectic as it is today.

We are fortunate that Frith was a photographer of the people, dedicated to recording the minutiae of everyday life. For it is this sheer wealth of visual data, the painstaking chronicle of changes in dress, transport, street layouts, buildings, housing, engineering and landscape that captivates us so much today. His remarkable images offer us a powerful link with the past and with the lives of our ancestors.

TODAY'S TECHNOLOGY

Computers have now made it possible for Frith's many thousands of images to be accessed almost instantly. In the Frith archive today, each photograph is carefully 'digitised' then stored on a CD Rom. Frith archivists can locate a single photograph amongst thousands within seconds. Views can be catalogued and sorted under a variety of categories of place and content to the immediate benefit of researchers. Inexpensive reference prints can be created for them at the touch of a mouse button, and a wide range of books and other printed materials assembled and published for a wider, more general readership - in the next twelve months over a hundred Frith local history titles will be published! The

THE FRANCIS FRITH COLLECTION
Photographic publishers since 1860

HOME | PHOTO SEARCH | BOOKS | PORTFOLIO | GALLERY   MY CART
Products | History | Other Collections | Contact us | Help?

your town,
your village

365,000
photographs of 7,000 towns and villages, taken between 1860 & 1970.

The Frith Archive
The Frith Archive is the remarkable legacy of its energetic and visionary founder. Today, the Frith archive is the only nationally important archive of its kind still in private ownership.

The Collection is world-renowned for the extraordinary quality of its images.

The Gallery
This month The Frith Gallery features images from "Frith's Egypt".

News...
Image update complete.
An additional 5,000 images have been added and the quality of all images has now been improved.

Sample Chapters available.
The first selection of sample chapters from the Frith Book Co.'s extensive range is now available. All are offered in Pdf format for easy downloading and viewing.

explore
FRITH

Search thousands of photographs from one of the worlds' great archives.

Town search
[   ] GO

County search
[Select a county ▾] GO

the **FRITHgallery**

See Frith at www.francisfrith.co.uk

day-to-day workings of the archive are very different from how they were in Francis Frith's time: imagine the herculean task of sorting through eleven tons of glass negatives as Frith had to do to locate a particular sequence of pictures! Yet the archive still prides itself on maintaining the same high standards of excellence laid down by Francis Frith, including the painstaking cataloguing and indexing of every view.

It is curious to reflect on how the internet now allows researchers in America and elsewhere greater instant access to the archive than Frith himself ever enjoyed. Many thousands of individual views can be called up on screen within seconds on one of the Frith internet sites, enabling people living continents away to revisit the streets of their ancestral home town, or view places in Britain where they have enjoyed holidays. Many overseas researchers welcome the chance to view special theme selections, such as transport, sports, costume and ancient monuments.

We are certain that Francis Frith would have heartily approved of these modern developments, for he himself was always working at the very limits of Victorian photographic technology.

THE VALUE OF THE ARCHIVE TODAY

Because of the benefits brought by the computer, Frith's images are increasingly studied by social historians, by researchers into genealogy and ancestory, by architects, town planners, and by teachers and schoolchildren involved in local history projects. In addition, the archive offers every one of us a unique opportunity to examine the places where we and our families have lived and worked down the years. Immensely successful in Frith's own era, the archive is now, a century and more on, entering a new phase of popularity.

THE PAST IN TUNE WITH THE FUTURE

Historians consider the Francis Frith Collection to be of prime national importance. It is the only archive of its kind remaining in private ownership and has been valued at a million pounds. However, this figure is now rapidly increasing as digital technology enables more and more people around the world to enjoy its benefits.

Francis Frith's archive is now housed in an historic timber barn in the beautiful village of Teffont in Wiltshire. Its founder would not recognize the archive office as it is today. In place of the many thousands of dusty boxes containing glass plate negatives and an all-pervading odour of photographic chemicals, there are now ranks of computer screens. He would be amazed to watch his images travelling round the world at unimaginable speeds through network and internet lines.

The archive's future is both bright and exciting. Francis Frith, with his unshakeable belief in making photographs available to the greatest number of people, would undoubtedly approve of what is being done today with his lifetime's work. His photographs, depicting our shared past, are now bringing pleasure and enlightenment to millions around the world a century and more after his death.

PENZANCE – *An Introduction*

PENZANCE STANDS ON the south-facing shores of Mount's Bay in the far west of Cornwall and within the regional district of Penwith. A market town and port, Penzance is also a holiday town, the gateway to the world-famous Land's End Peninsula, one of the most inspiring areas in Britain. Mount's Bay is named after the spectacular island of St Michael's Mount, that stands just offshore from Penzance's neighbouring town of Marazion. It is the largest bay in England. Behind Penzance the ancient hills of Penwith, a name that in Cornish means 'the farthest end', rise through a charming landscape of small fields and shady woods to where prehistoric remains punctuate the heather and gorse-clad moorland of the peninsula.

Penzance began life as a small fishing settlement on a rocky headland that protrudes into Mount's Bay. First records of the name Pensans appeared in the late 13th century. There have been various interpretations proposed for the name. These range from 'head of the bay' to 'the saint's head', but most authorities agree on the simple translation of 'holy headland' from the Cornish pen, meaning 'head' or 'end', and sans, meaning 'holy'.

This name may have derived from the presence of a small chapel dedicated to St Anthony of Padua, which stood on the shore near the town's present day St Anthony Gardens.

ANCIENT PENZANCE

The earliest relics of human habitation in Penzance are at Lescudjack Hill, just inland from the town centre. Here stood an Iron Age fortification, typical of many throughout the Land's End Peninsula, and dating from a time when tribal conflicts over land and trade resulted in a more aggressive way of life. It is not certain that the Romans reached as far west of Penzance, although Roman artifacts have been found in the area. What is known is that this far western land remained outside the major developments of post-Roman Britain. Saxon overlordship certainly extended as far as the Penwith district. The name Alverton Street in present day Penzance derives from the name of a Saxon overlord called Alward, who was dispossessed of his manor after the Norman Conquest of 1066. Yet in spite of Saxon and then Norman influence, the old way of life of this far western district survived, and gives to Penzance and its environs a separate identity from the rest of England.

Penzance first appears as a medieval settlement in records of the 13th century. For the next hundred years or so the town was in competition with its neighbouring settlements of Marazion and Mousehole over which would be the main port and market of Mount's Bay. Marazion was initially of greater

days of Drake and the Spanish Armada were over, but Spanish raiders based in Brittany still harried the south-west coast of Britain. On 23 July 1595 a force of Spanish soldiers landed from four galleys near Mousehole on the southern edge of Mount's Bay. The Spaniards set fire to Mousehole and to the village of Paul on the hill above. They then moved on to Penzance along the low shoreline, driving back a hastily gathered force of defenders. The Spaniards burned and looted Penzance

importance than either Penzance or Mousehole. All three settlements entered the 16th century vying with each other over the relative importance of their chapels, harbours and markets.

SPANISH RAIDERS

By the end of the 16th century, Penzance's fortunes were at a low ebb. Marazion was incorporated as a borough by Queen Elizabeth I. Barely had this municipal triumph over Penzance been ratified than the old enemy Spain delivered a far more savage blow to the 'Holy Headland'. The famous

before returning to their ships. By the time reinforcements had gathered on land and British naval ships reached Mount's Bay, the Spaniards had sailed off on favourable winds.

Undaunted by the setback of the Spanish Raid, the medieval traders and merchants of Penzance redoubled their efforts to become the leading port of Mount's Bay. A combination of clever and ruthless business tactics led to Penzance receiving its Charter of Incorporation as a Borough from King James I on 9 May, 1614. Soon Penzance had overtaken Marazion as a market town, and the latter's fortunes declined. But Marazion remains a borough to this day, an ancient town proud of its history and with the spectacular nearby island of St. Michael's Mount adding to its deserved popularity with visitors.

TIN TOWN

Throughout the 17th and 18th centuries, Penzance prospered as a market town and as a port. Cornwall was a major centre of pilchard fishing during this time and much of Penzance's trade was in the export of salted fish, chiefly to the Mediterranean. Trade with France gave Penzance even more colourful connections. The history of the town is linked inextricably with the history of smuggling; it seems likely that the port was as much engaged in 'free trade' as it was in legitimate business. In the mid 17th century Penzance received a commercial boost when it was made a 'Coinage Town', one of the privileged centres where tin was assayed by having a corner or 'coin' removed from a shipment in order to check its quality before it was sold and exported. This led to Penzance becoming an industrial and financial centre of the mining industry. With the advantage of a busy harbour and lucrative markets, Penzance prospered throughout the 18th century and entered the 19th century as a self-confident and thriving borough.

During the 19th century great progress was made in developing Penzance's harbour, and by the last quarter of the century the town still profited from its traditional connections with the sea and with mineral mining. It was also a busy market town. This was an economic fabric that might eventually have unravelled because of changes in commercial and industrial conditions; but in the run-up to the new world of the 20th century, Penzance benefited enormously from one of the greatest developments of the industrial age, the railway.

RAILWAY REVOLUTION

During the early 19th century, any extension of the railway to the far west of England had

been piecemeal. Mineral railways were part of Cornwall's mining industry from the earliest years of the century, but it was only in the 1850s that a railway line was opened between Penzance and Truro. By 1849 trains were running between London and Plymouth. Brunel's railway bridge over the Tamar was opened in 1859, and now the last great obstacle to expansion westwards was overcome. Different gauges on the various connected lines meant that Penzance was not finally linked to London on a through line until 1866, when it became the south west terminus of one of the great railway lines of Victorian Britain. This rail link with London was of huge value to Penzance. It meant that perishable products such as fish from the Cornish seas and early flowers and potatoes from the farms could be transported to major markets within a day. The traffic was two-way, but the return traffic was in human form: the fast-developing tourist industry brought more and more visitors to the far west, to the irresistible attraction of Land's End and to the new leisure activity of sea bathing.

TWENTIETH CENTURY TOWN

The early decades of the 20th century saw Penzance share in the ups and downs of a changing world in which local decisions and local economics had less impact than in the days of poor communications. The town's old industries of sea trade and mining declined, but farming remained healthy and tourism grew apace. The story of Penzance in the latter half of the 20th century was one of consolidation. In 1974, when the Local Government Act of 1972 came into force, the borough of Penzance lost much of its executive power, which was taken over by a new District Council of Penwith. Today Penwith Council has its offices in Penzance, and council meetings are held in Penzance's town hall, the handsome granite building in Alverton Street known as St John's Hall. During the 1980s and 1990s Penzance went through some difficult times, but at the Millennium this delightful little town in its magnificent setting by the sea remains full of sunny charm.

PENZANCE
A Distant View 1908 61226

The Town

WHEN PENZANCE was raided by Spanish forces in 1595, the town's harbour area was destroyed, robbing the modern Penzance of medieval buildings that might otherwise have survived to this day. Few buildings have survived from the 17th century either, but two thatched houses on the road to Land's End, one at Tredarvah and one at Hawk's Farm, are thought to date from the late 17th century, although they have been renovated over the years. The handsome manor house of Trereife on the western outskirts of Penzance may also date from the late 17th century.

It was during the 18th century that the character of Penzance's central sea front and of streets like Chapel Street evolved. Many of the finest houses in Chapel Street are built of brick instead of the local granite common in West Cornwall. This may reflect Penzance's 18th century contacts with a wider world that influenced fashion in architecture. The Victorian era saw further prosperity for Penzance. It was during this period that many of the more substantial public and private buildings that still enhance the town were built. Penzance's Regency character is due to the number of handsome terraces constructed during the first decades of the 19th century. Their stuccoed and painted walls impart a smooth elegance to the architecture of the town. This makes a pleasing contrast to the rough texture of the native granite used in many of Penzance's older houses and in such handsome structures as the Market House in Market Place, the Public Buildings in Alverton Street and the Parish Church of St Mary above the harbour.

The main street of Penzance is Market Jew Street, a busy shopping area with a flanking terrace that leads gently uphill to the handsome classical building of the Market House. Behind Market House is Market Place, from where the other shopping streets of Causewayhead and Alverton Street lead off. From Market Place the charming Chapel Street winds down to the harbour between attractive buildings that include the lavishly painted and ornamented Egyptian House, the 14th century Turk's Head Inn, the Admiral Benbow restaurant and the final flourish of the tall tower of the Church of St Mary.

Penzance's south-facing aspect and mild climate has nurtured the subtropical Morrab Gardens and the peaceful Penlee Memorial Park. Both lie between the centre of the town and the sea front. It is in the colourful floral displays of Morrab Gardens, together with the Gardens' 'Cornish Riviera' palm trees, that the unique character of Penzance is vividly expressed. Here is a town blessed by its position and enhanced by buildings that are in proportion with its size and in keeping with the style of its surroundings, a town that still retains some of the atmosphere of its colourful and accomplished past.

MORRAB GARDENS C1955 P40059
Band performances at the Band Stand in Penzance's famous Morrab Gardens have delighted audiences for many years before and after this photograph was taken. Note the palm trees, enduring symbols of the Cornish Riviera.

MORRAB GARDENS 1906 56517
Ladies enjoying the sunshine beside the War Memorial that stands in front of Morrab House Library. The originally private gardens were bought as a public park by Penzance Corporation in 1888.

MORRAB GARDENS c1960 P40136
This photograph shows one of the fine views from Morrab Gardens looking towards Mount's Bay with Penlee Point in the distance. The fountain has stood on this site for more than a hundred years.

THE PARISH CHURCH c1955 P40089
This photograph shows St Mary's Church on its elevated site at the bottom of Chapel Street. Its tall tower makes it a significant landmark. It was built in 1832 on the site of the medieval St. Mary's Chapel.

St Mary's Parish Church 1906 56519
A fire in 1985 caused extensive damage to the church, and to special features such as the marble high altar shown here. Repair work took more than two years to complete and cost nearly half a million pounds.

THE GARDEN OF REMEMBRANCE c1955 P40072

THE MERMAID THEATRE c1955 P40073

THE GARDEN OF REMEMBRANCE c1955
A photograph of Penzance's Garden of Remembrance in the peaceful Penlee Park, behind the Penlee House Art Gallery and Museum.

◆

THE MERMAID THEATRE c1955
This photograph shows the grass-covered stage of the delightful outdoor Memorial Theatre in Penzance's Penlee Park, which is used today for a variety of performances.

ST JOHN THE BAPTIST CHURCH 1908 61236
The church was built in 1880; it was named after the motif of the Baptist's head on a platter that was adopted as the town seal of Penance in 1614, a punning reference to Penzance's name deriving from the Cornish words for 'Holy Headland'.

CHAPEL YARD 1908 59461
Chapel Court is situated at the top of Quay Street, the street that leads up from Penzance Harbour. The houses are long gone, but the wall on the left of the picture is the wall of Chapel House, now Penzance Arts Club, and can still be seen today.

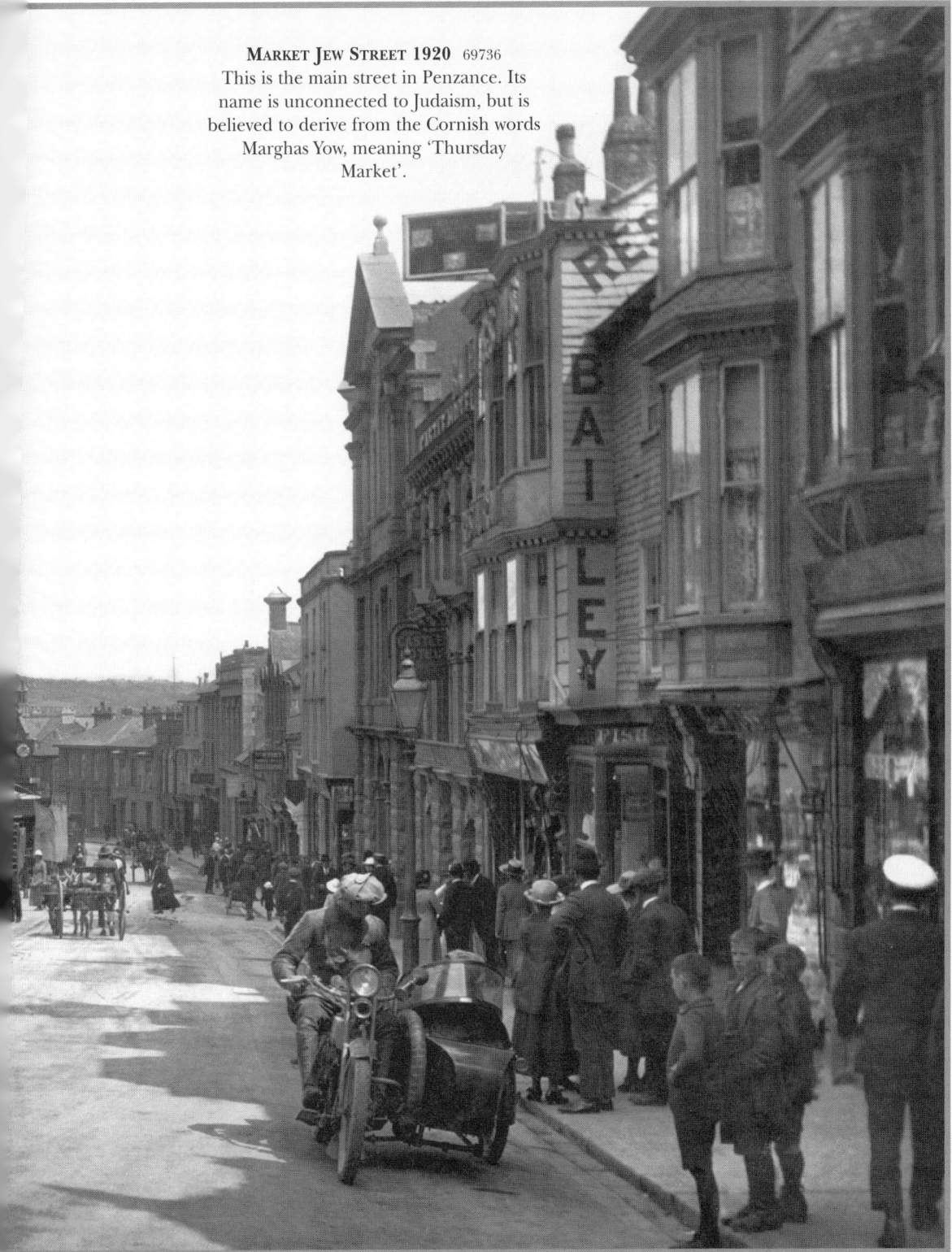

MARKET JEW STREET 1920 69736
This is the main street in Penzance. Its name is unconnected to Judaism, but is believed to derive from the Cornish words Marghas Yow, meaning 'Thursday Market'.

MARKET JEW STREET 1925 78635
The handsome building with Ionic portico is
the Market House, built in 1838 to replace an
original Market House that had been
demolished two years earlier.

MARKET JEW STREET C1955 P40079

The statue is of the famous scientist Sir Humphry Davy, who was born in 1778 in one of the houses on the right hand side of the picture. Davy invented a miners' safety lamp and identified nitrous oxide, 'laughing gas'.

MARKET JEW STREET C1955 P40083

The raised pavement, known locally as 'The Terrace', can be clearly seen on the left hand side of the road. The terrace is paved with huge granite slabs.

ALVERTON STREET 1908 61232
Looking along the main road into Penzance from the west. Bellair, a fine Regency house, once stood in the area to the right. The building was destroyed by bombs during the Second World War, and on its site now stands the Area Health Clinic

THE GREENMARKET 1925 78636
This view shows Timothy White's Household Stores, which remained on this corner until the 1960s. The building on the right was originally the Public Benefit Boot Company. It dates from 1905, and is built of red and cream bricks, a fashionable style of the time.

THE GREENMARKET c1955 P40105
This photograph looks from the Greenmarket towards the dome of the Market House, a well-known Penzance landmark. The dome contains a large circular room, from the windows of which there are extensive views.

THE SQUARE c1960

The central building in this picture is Penzance Market House. It was originally the Town Hall and market. Lloyds Bank has occupied this western end of the building since 1925. The entire building was bought by Lloyds in 1965.

THE TOWN HALL c1955

The Town Hall is situated in Alverton Street. Known locally as St John's Hall, the building dates from 1867. The top step of the entrance is a huge slab of granite measuring nearly six metres by one metre, and is said to be the largest piece of cut granite in the world.

THE SQUARE c1960   P40146

THE TOWN HALL c1955   P40077

The Harbour

THE HARBOUR was the main reason for Penzance's existence from earliest times, but during the 20th century, as the commercial importance of seagoing declined, and as the local fishing industry became concentrated at the neighbouring port of Newlyn, Penzance's harbour lost some of its viability. A sign of the changing times came in 1968, when a large part of the tidal harbour was filled in to provide land for a car park.

Things were very different during the 19th century, when development of the harbour was of paramount importance. Various schemes for enlarging and improving the harbour emerged in the 1830s, and by 1848 a new pier, the Albert Pier, had been built. This pier, together with the existing South Pier, enclosed and gave some protection to a large area of tidal water. Roads in the harbour area were improved. The tidal nature of Penzance Harbour meant that vessels went aground during the periods of low tide, always a great handicap for a harbour with commercial aspirations. At certain low tide periods, large vessels still have difficulty in entering Penzance Harbour, although the MV 'Scillonian III', the ferry that runs between Penzance and the Isles of Scilly, over 30 miles to the south west, operates successfully from the seaward end of the South Pier.

The problem of Penzance Harbour's tidal nature was tackled in the 1880s with a scheme that would provide the harbour with an inner dock where tidal water could be impounded behind lock gates. This would allow large vessels to remain afloat at all times, although their coming and going would still be limited to high tide when the lock gates were opened. This inner dock was operative by 1884; it remains an important feature, an increasingly well-used haven for fishing boats, commercial vessels and visiting yachts.

Another important feature of the harbour was its dry dock, a specially constructed basin into which vessels manoeuvred at high tide. The water was then pumped out so that work could be carried out on the vessel's hull as well as its superstructure. There had been a dry dock at the inner corner of Penzance Harbour in the early 19th century, but a more substantial facility was opened in 1880. Access to the dry dock is through a swing bridge, the Ross Bridge, across which the harbour front road still runs.

Today, from Easter to October, Penzance's outer harbour is filled with yacht and motor boat moorings and the sight of yachts coming and going, a sign of the town's vigorous sailing community and of the increasing importance of leisure sailing. Within the granite-walled inner dock, larger fishing boats and commercial vessels load and unload; in summer visiting yachts and the occasional tall-masted sailing ship lie against the quays. Close to the harbour is the unique Trinity House National Lighthouse Centre with its fascinating exhibitions and displays.

In the new world of the 21st century, and with calls for a yacht marina and other developments, Penzance Harbour and its seagoing community seem destined once more to become a major feature of the town, whose very development arose because of its potential as a port.

THE HARBOUR 1893 31783
This view looks towards St. Michael's Mount. The harbour is protected from prevailing westerly winds, but is exposed to gales from the south and east. Penzance Harbour is tidal, and much of the muddy bed of the harbour is exposed for a few hours at low tide.

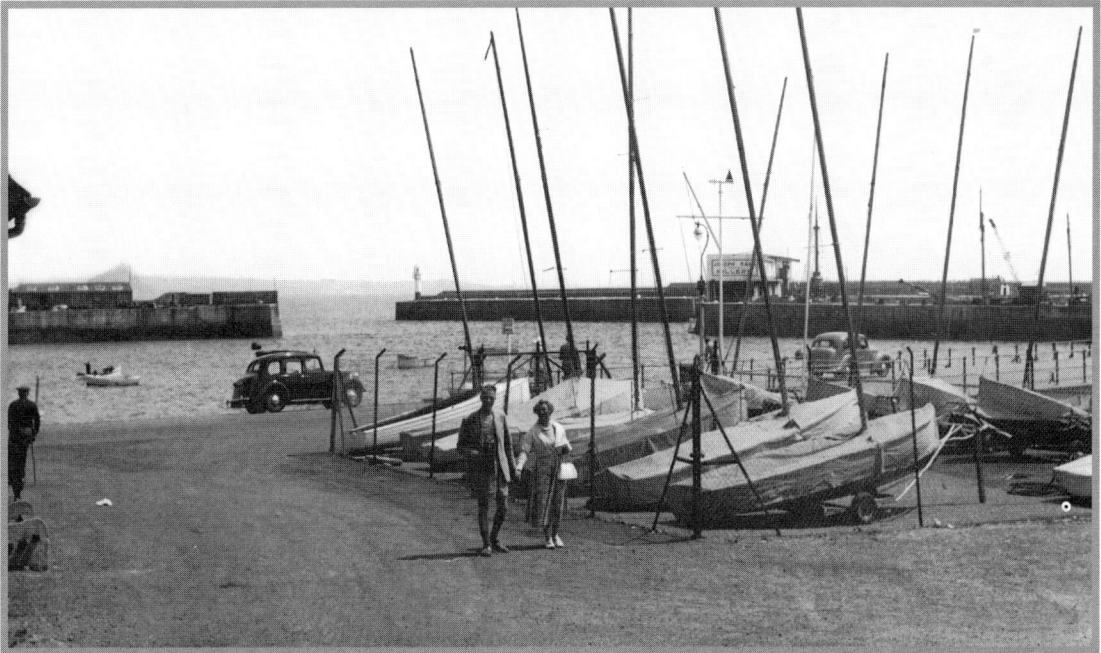

THE HARBOUR c1960 P40111
Looking across the harbour from the dinghy pen at the bottom of Jennings Street. The area is now paved and is further enhanced by attractive flower beds and seating.

THE HARBOUR 1893 31777
The original pier, known as South Pier, is in the
background. In 1845 work started on the pier
seen in the foreground. It was named Albert Pier
after Queen Victoria's consort, Prince Albert,
who landed at the unfinished pier in 1846 on an
official visit to Penzance.

THE HARBOUR c1960 P40122

This photograph was taken before a large part of the tidal area was filled in with rubble to create a car park. The building on the left of the harbour is the Penzance Gas Works, which was demolished some years later and is now the site of the Wharfside shopping complex.

THE HARBOUR 1890 22974

By the middle of the 19th century, it was realised that Penzance needed a protected inner dock that could accommodate larger trading vessels. After many financial and construction problems, this inner dock, the gates of which are pictured here, was completed in 1884.

TORPEDO BOATS IN THE HARBOUR c1955 P40071

**TORPEDO BOATS
THE HARBOUR c1955**
Penzance's inner dock is still a busy and interesting place where all types of vessels, from cargo ships to fishing boats, modern yachts to sailing ships, lie alongside its quays. This photograph records a visit to Penzance by Royal Naval Torpedo boats.

◆

THE HARBOUR c1965
A view of the inner dock. Quite large boats can enter the harbour at high tide. At high tide, the dock gates are closed and the water retained so as to keep vessels afloat at all times within the dock.

THE HARBOUR c1965 P40155

FISHING BOATS 1890 22978A
The harbourside Wharf Road was constructed in
1866. It made life much easier for harbour users
by improving communication to the harbour area
and by increasing facilities for the loading and
unloading of vessels.

RMS SCILLONIAN c1955 P40054

Looking across the crowded decks of the Penzance-Isles of Scilly ferry, 'Scillonian I'. At the far side of the harbour is Ross Bridge, a swing bridge, built in the previous century, and modernised in the late 20th century. It enabled large vessels to enter the dry dock at Penzance.

THE HARBOUR c1955 P40065

A view from Abbey Slip, looking across Ross Bridge to the harbour at high tide. The partially enclosed area of water in the foreground gave vessels room to manoeuvre while entering Penzance's dry dock, which lies to the right of the picture.

THE 'SCILLONIAN' 1925 78637

THE 'SCILLONIAN' 1925
The very first Penzance-Isles of Scilly ferry, MV 'Scillonian I', pictured here during its first year of service. Subsequent vessels of the Isles of Scilly Steamship Company have carried cargo and passengers to and from the Islands.

◆

THE 'SCILLONIAN' 1955
MV 'Scillonian I' is moored against the South Pier during her last year of service. The lighthouse which can be seen at the end of the pier had already been standing for a hundred years, and is still in use today.

THE 'SCILLONIAN' 1955 P40055

THE SCILLY BOAT 1927 79944

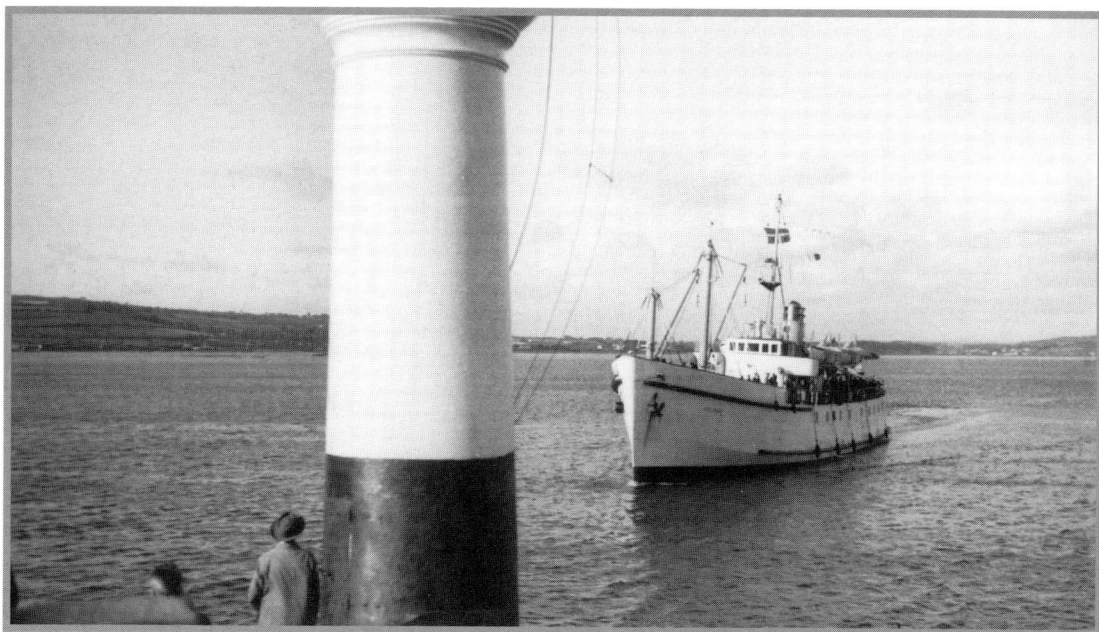

THE 'SCILLONIAN' c1960 P40130

The Penzance-Isles of Scilly ferry 'Scillonian II' approaching Penzance harbour. She was replaced by the present 'Scillonian III' in 1977. The 'Scillonian III' has since carried well over a million passengers between Penzance and the Isles of Scilly and is still in operation.

QUAY STREET 1906 56515

Looking from Penzance Harbour up Quay Street towards St Mary's Church. The medieval buildings that once stood here were destroyed by Spanish raiders in 1595.

JENNINGS STREET c1965 P40110
Jennings Street is one of the streets that links Market Jew Street to Wharf Road on Penzance's harbour front. The terrace of cottages on the left was demolished soon after this photograph was taken.

VIEW FROM MARKET JEW STREET c1965 P40147
Looking down Albert Street to Penzance Harbour car-park. This was once part of the harbour, but the area was filled in to accommodate some of the huge number of vehicles which come to Penance during the summer months.

The Promenade

PENZANCE PROMENADE is famed as being the longest in Cornwall. It is certainly one of the most invigorating seaside walkways in Britain, nearly half a mile of broad open paving unencumbered with buildings and flanked by the great expanse of Mount's Bay to the sunny south. Built in 1844, the promenade lay along the line of the Western Green, an area of sand dunes and grassy hills. The promenade was known also as the Marine Esplanade in the best traditions of the day.

Tourism was in its infancy when the Promenade was built, but its existence seemed an emphatic statement that the town authorities believed that the future lay with 'visitors'. The Promenade certainly marked a dramatic and ironic end to the dominance of the local fishing industry, an industry that was romanticised through the marvellous paintings of the Newlyn School artists of the late 19th century and which is seen as such a colourful part of Cornwall's heritage today. In the early 19th century, fishing was seen as too intrusive for tourism. The Western Green had long been the preserve of fishing and seafaring. Boats were drawn up on the sand, fishermen landed fish on the beaches at low tide, and nets were spread out to dry on the grassy dunes. But by the 1860s fishermen were prohibited from using the promenade for drying their nets, because tourists complained that boats were passing in front of bathing machines while the machines were in use.

The Promenade has received some hard treatment from the sea throughout the years.

Penzance's foreshore is vulnerable to gales from the south and east, and when such gales occur during very high tides, the effect on the promenade, and at times the buildings along the sea front, has been devastating. In 1895 a storm caused great damage to the Promenade, and large areas had to be renewed. The railings on the Promenade's lower terrace were also removed over the years. A huge storm in 1962 caused so much damage that virtually the entire Promenade was rebuilt, this time with a dynamically curved sea-facing wall aimed at dampening and deflecting the often explosive impact of storm waves.

One of the great features of Penzance's sea front is the open-air Jubilee Pool, which lies at the eastern end of the Promenade just beyond the inner harbour. The Pool is an excellent example of the art deco style of 1930s marine architecture. Public concern over the pool's structural decay during the 1980s led to the pool being saved from demolition after strong campaigning in its favour by local people. The pool has since been refurbished. In spite of such important facilities, the Promenade was never heavily developed, although various buildings, bandstands and other features have come and gone. On the inner side of the road, near the western end of the Promenade, is the old Pavilion Theatre; it was built in 1911 and is now an amusement arcade and restaurant. Today, with many of its finest features still intact, Penzance Promenade is still a superb facility.

THE PROMENADE 1893 31778A
Penzance's original promenade was built in 1844. The lower section still exists, but its railings are now gone. In 1895 a storm caused so much structural damage to the promenade that sections had to be rebuilt.

THE PROMENADE 1897 40598C

A storm lashes the Promenade. It has always been extremely vulnerable to south-easterly gales. When the monthly 'spring' tides occur, the highest tides in the cycle, the combined force of high water and high winds can be devastating.

THE PROMENADE 1908 60982B
In 1962 a huge storm caused so much damage to Penzance Promenade that most of it had to be rebuilt, this time with a curved sea defence wall, which has survived subsequent batterings by the sea.

THE ESPLANADE C1883 16022
This view looks towards the fishing village of Newlyn. The buildings on the right are The Mount's Bay Hotel and the Queen's Hotel. Both date from the 1860s, and were built to accommodate the flood of tourists arriving on the newly opened railway line between London and Penzance.

THE QUEEN'S HOTEL 1897 40602
The Queen's has been one of Penzance's
leading hotels for well over a hundred years.

THE PROMENADE 1906 56508
'Promenading' was a popular pastime for many
generations of Penzance people, particularly on a
Sunday. The newly constructed band-stand seen in
the middle distance was an important meeting
point. It was demolished during the rebuilding of
the promenade after storm damage in the 1960s.

SOUTH TERRACE 1890 27694
Old-style transport is seen in this view along South Terrace at the eastern end of the Promenade. The tower of St Mary's Church can be seen in the background.

THE PROMENADE 1924 76646
This hotel still stands at the junction of Alexandra Road and the western end of Penzance Promenade. The ornate buildings in the background incorporated the 'Bijou House', and were typical of seaside architecture of the time. They were demolished some years later.

THE BEACH 1927 79940
This view looks towards Newlyn. The Bijou House closed off this end of the promenade where a car park now stands.

THE PROMENADE c1955 P40060
Looking towards Penzance's Jubilee Bathing Pool. The attractive row of cottages and gardens, Marine Terrace, looks out across Mount's Bay. Each house is different from its neighbour, a variety that adds to the terrace's charm.

FROM THE BATHING PLACE 1893 31780

FROM THE BATHING PLACE 1893
This photograph was taken looking westward from the rocks known as the Bathing Place, a site which later became the location of the Jubilee Bathing Pool.

◆

THE BATHING POOL 1935
A view looking across the Jubilee Pool towards St Mary's Parish Church. In front of the church is the imposing Coinage Hall, built in 1816. The building later became a Seamen's Institute, then a language school; it is now private residences.

THE BATHING POOL 1935 86860

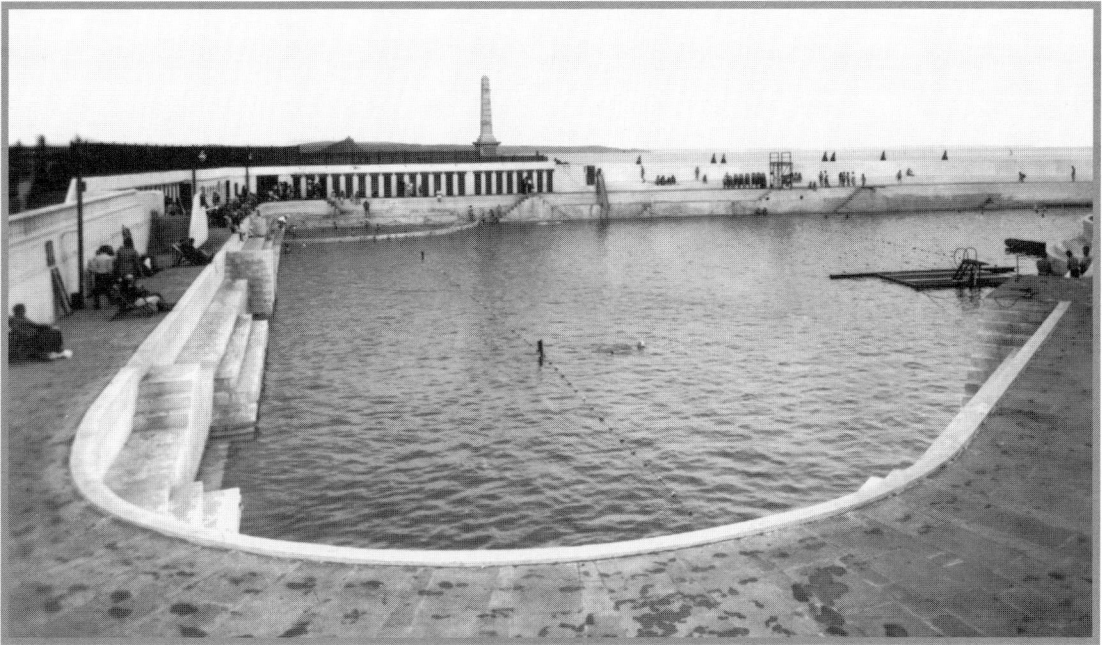

THE SWIMMING POOL c1955 P40091
The Jubilee Pool, built in distinctive art deco style, was completed in 1935. It is now a listed building, and its survival has been the result of strong local campaigning against its demolition.

THE SWIMMING POOL c1960 P40149
The pool has been popular with locals and visitors during the summer months for more than sixty years. In 1999 the pool had major refurbishment carried out.

THE BEACH 1927 79938
Generations of Penzance youngsters have
explored rock pools on the tidal foreshore.
This photograph captures the fascination and
concentration of 'rock pooling' at low tide.

THE TENNIS COURTS 1920 69734

Looking across the Promenade tennis courts to the bowling green. St Mary's Church of England School is on the left. In the background is the Pavilion Theatre, which had opened nine years earlier. The theatre building now houses an amusement arcade and restaurant.

ON THE ROCKS 1906 56513

These rocks were the site of the remarkable Wherrytown tin mine, whose shaft could only be worked at low tides. The mine was begun in 1778; though it produced tin ore, it was abandoned eventually in 1840.

THE SANDS 1920 69732
This beach scene is complete with bathing machines. During the 19th century the beach was used for the sale of fish, and fishing boats lay on the sand at low tide.

THE BEACH 1927 79942

By the 1920s Penzance had become a popular holiday resort, as this busy scene shows. Many people travelled to the town by the Great Western Railway. Holidaymakers even travelled by steamer from London, Liverpool, Glasgow and Portsmouth to Plymouth, and then boarded the Penzance train there.

THE BEDFORD BOLITHO GARDENS 1924 76648

These splendid gardens were situated at the western end of the Promenade. Complete with terraces, shelters and picturesque flower beds, the gardens were a popular spot, not least because of the fine views of Mount's Bay.

THE BEDFORD BOLITHO GARDENS 1920 69738

THE BEDFORD BOLITHO GARDENS 1920
The gardens were frequently damaged by storms because of their exposed position on the sea front. The 'Great Storm' of 1962 caused so much damage to the gardens that it was decided to demolish them and to replace them with a car park.

◆

THE WAR MEMORIAL 1924
This photograph shows the newly-erected war memorial at Battery Rocks at the eastern end of the Promenade. The rocks were so named because of the small fort , armed with cannons, that was placed there in 1740 because of fears of attack by French forces.

THE WAR MEMORIAL 1924 76650

ST ANTHONY'S GARDENS AND BATHING POOL 1935 86859
A fine view looking down across St Anthony's Gardens to the newly constructed Jubilee Bathing Pool.

ST ANTHONY'S GARDENS AND PROMENADE c1955 P40063
The gardens date from the 1930s. They are named after St Anthony's Chapel, a medieval chapel that once stood nearby, which may have been named after St Anthony of Padua, patron saint of fishermen.

ST ANTHONY'S GARDENS c1955 P40107
The gardens are complete with typical Penzance palm trees. St Michael's Mount can be seen in the distance across the bay.

Around and About

PENZANCE is blessed with magnificent surroundings in virtually all directions. The town is the true gateway to the Land's End Peninsula, the final outpost of West Cornwall before the Atlantic takes over. It is a peninsula world-renowned for its spectacular sea cliffs, its wild and beautiful coastline and for the beauty of its moorlands, where the haunting remains of prehistoric burial chambers such as the famous Lanyon Quoit bear witness to an ancient past. Even in roadside fields you will find prehistoric standing stones or stone circles, such as the Rosemodress Circle to the south of Penzance. This circle is known popularly as the Merry Maidens; this name comes from much later myths of local girls being turned to stone as punishment for dancing on the Sabbath. The true purpose of such evocative memorials is not entirely clear, but their significance to their Neolithic-Bronze Age builders was probably as ceremonial sites.

The coast to the south and west of Penzance is one of the loveliest in Britain. Along the granite seashore, where golden daffodils bloom in spring and where a riot of flowers turn the cliff sides into wild gardens in early summer, lie narrow wooded valleys such as Lamorna. Here, old stone-built waterfalls harnessed the valley stream and at Lamorna Cove granite quarrying was once a busy industry. Today, Lamorna is deeply wooded. The old quarries have become wild nature reserves and the beautiful seaward cove is a hugely popular tourist venue, all signs of a greatly changed world from that of a century ago.

Closer to Penzance itself lie a string of charming Cornish villages, Paul, Madron and Gulval. These villages are closely linked to the town, yet have retained unique identities in their old buildings, country inns and splendid granite churches. More substantial is the fishing village of Newlyn, located to the west of Penzance in a corner of Mount's Bay that is protected from prevailing westerly winds. Newlyn and Penzance have always retained their individuality, and the long open expanse of Penzance Promenade and its airy continuation of grassy open space along the foreshore to Newlyn maintains that individuality.

It takes only a few minutes to drive from the centre of Penzance into a countryside which is engagingly Cornish, a countryside of stone walls, small fields and quiet woods, beyond which lies open moorland swathed in purple heather and yellow gorse. With all of this, and with one of the finest outlooks of any town in Britain, Penzance remains as appealing as ever.

GULVAL, THE OLD INN 1893 31790

Gulval is located just to the east of Penzance. The Old Inn stood opposite Gulval's handsome granite church. The site on which the original inn stood is now the site of The Coldstreamer inn.

GULVAL, THE CHURCH 1893 31791

A fine view of Penzance from above Gulval church. Gulval became part of the borough of Penzance when the borough boundaries were extended in 1934.

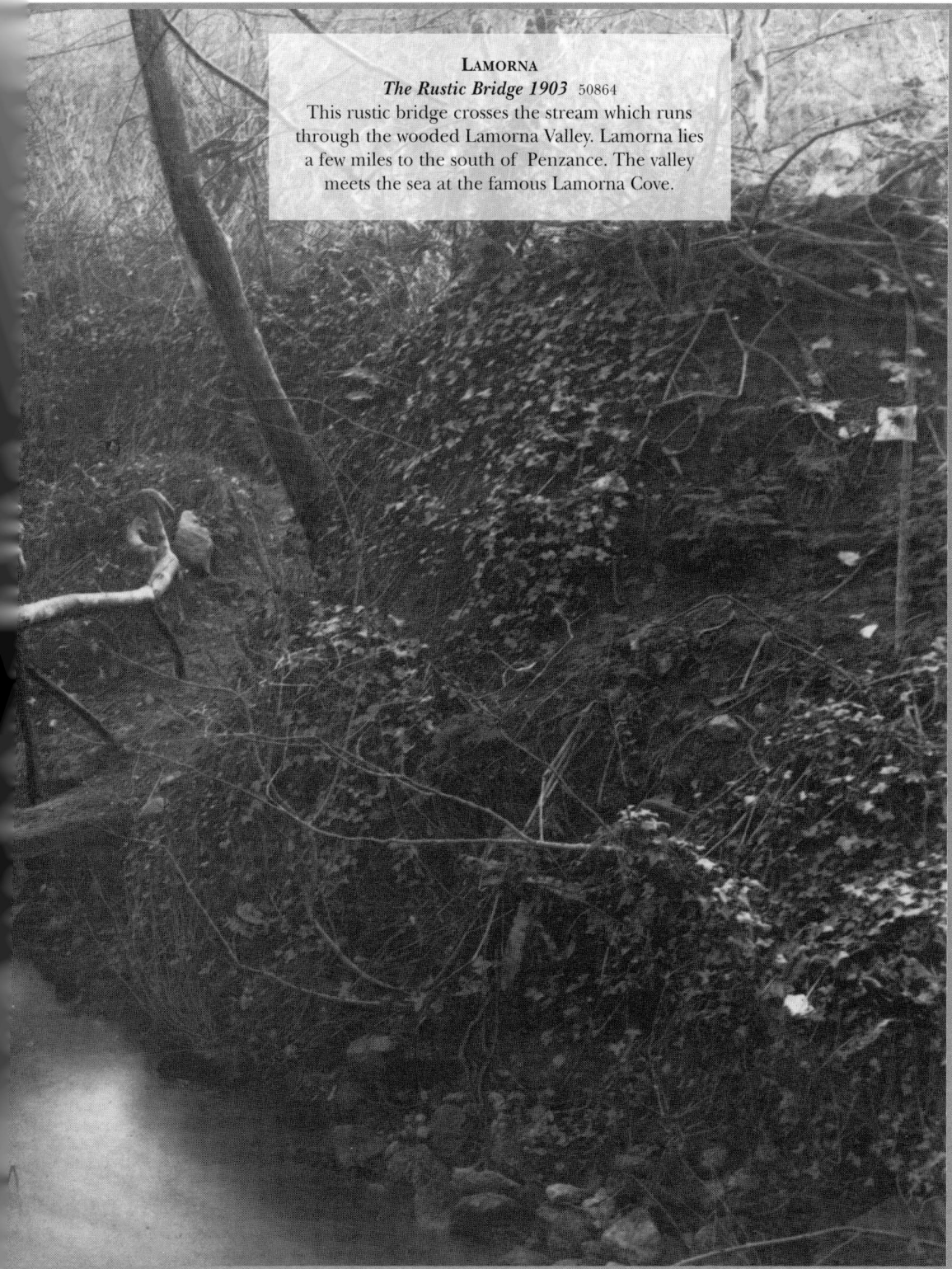

LAMORNA
The Rustic Bridge 1903 50864
This rustic bridge crosses the stream which runs through the wooded Lamorna Valley. Lamorna lies a few miles to the south of Penzance. The valley meets the sea at the famous Lamorna Cove.

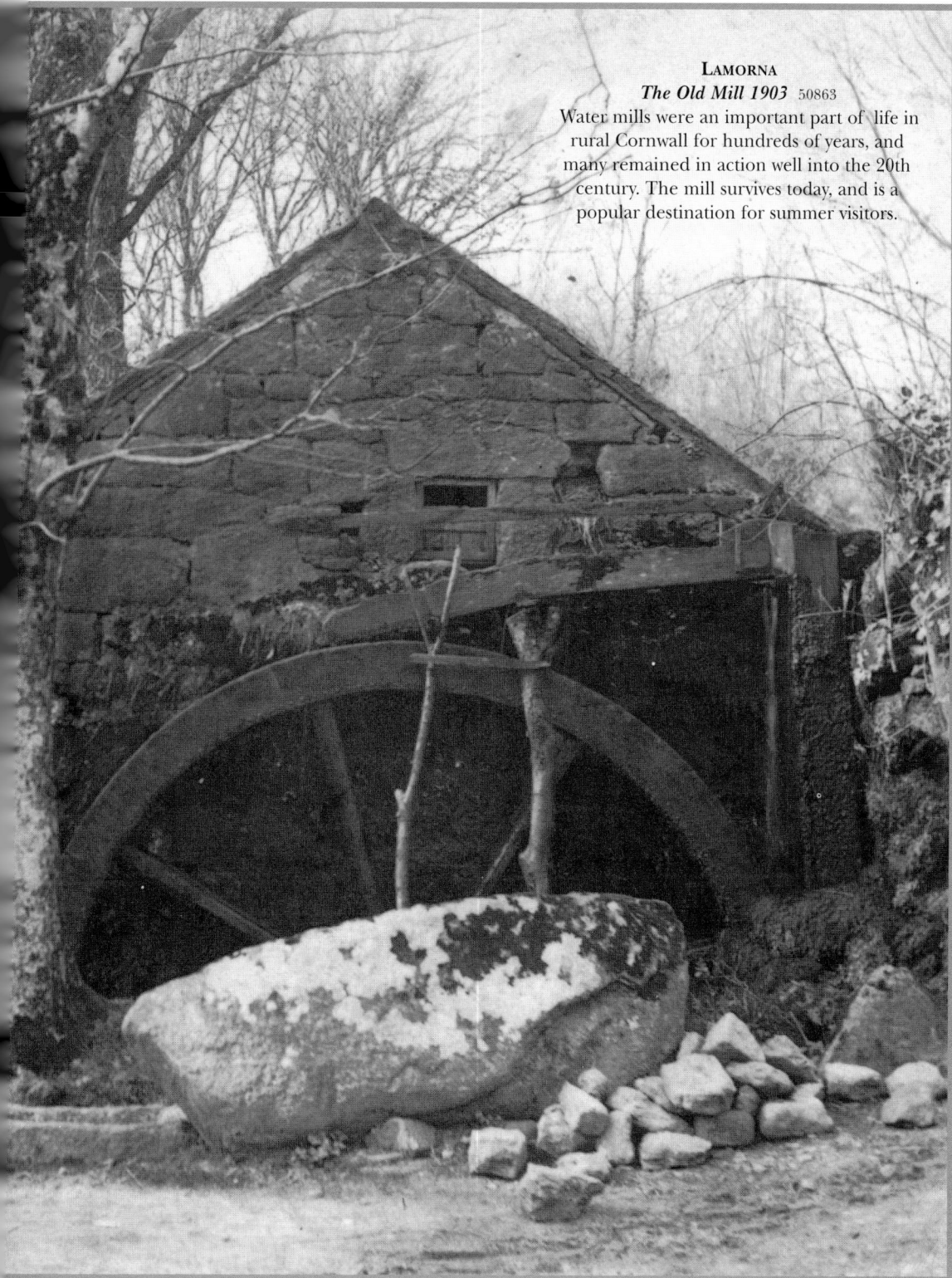

LAMORNA
The Old Mill 1903 50863
Water mills were an important part of life in rural Cornwall for hundreds of years, and many remained in action well into the 20th century. The mill survives today, and is a popular destination for summer visitors.

TREDARVAH FARM 1908 59460

TREDARVAH FARM 1908
No longer a farm today, Tredarvah is situated on the main A30 road which leads out of Penzance to the west. It is one of only a few thatched houses in the area to survive, and is believed to date back to the late 17th century.

TREREIFE HOUSE c1955
Trereife House stands about a mile to the west of Penzance. The facade is a fine example of the Queen Anne style executed in granite, and dates from the early 18th century.

TREREIFE HOUSE c1955 P40086

THE STONE CIRCLE c1955 P40076

The 'Merry Maidens' is an early Bronze Age ceremonial site near Lamorna to the south west of Penzance. Its 'Merry Maidens' name is a much later invention, and comes from local myths about young girls being turned to stone as punishment for dancing on Sunday.

LANYON QUOIT c1960 P40501

This ancient Neolithic monument lies between Penzance and the village of Morvah on the north coast of the Land's End Peninsula. The 'quoit' or 'cromlech' is the interior stone chamber of an ancient burial mound; the earth and stones which covered it have long disappeared.

PENZANCE HELIPORT c1965 P40140

Penzance Heliport is pictured not long after its opening in 1964 on the outskirts of the town. It is used by helicopters flying the twenty-minute trip between the Isles of Scilly and the mainland.

MADRON CHURCH 1920 69742

The church, school house and war memorial at the village of Madron, two miles north of Penzance. Penzance was originally part of the parish of Madron. The splendid church of St. Madernus dates in part from the 14th century.

FROM NEWLYN 1920 69726

This view from the top of Paul Hill is as spectacular today as it was when the photograph was taken. Paul Hill is a notoriously steep hill that rises from sea level at Newlyn to the higher ground of the Land's End Peninsula.

GENERAL VIEW 1895 36168

Looking towards Newlyn Harbour and Penlee Point. At this time Newlyn is said to have had a fleet of four hundred boats involved in pilchard and mackerel fishing.

THE GARDENS c1960 P40116
A view of Newlyn from the large open area fringing the sea at the eastern approach to the village.

PENLEE GARDENS 1920 69740
Looking towards Newlyn from the Bedford Bolitho Gardens, now known as the Bolitho Gardens. Just above the beach there is a paved walkway that leads to Newlyn from the end of the promenade at Penzance.

NEWLYN, VILLAGE SCENE 1903 49956
The cottages, in what is now Gwavas Road, were later demolished to make way for the present Newlyn Centenary Methodist Church of 1927. The political campaigner and social reformer William Lovett, one of the founders of the 19th century Chartist movement, lived in one of the cottages in his youth.

NEWLYN, FISHERMEN'S COTTAGES 1906 56526
A scene that might well have been posed for a painting with all the trappings of a fisherman's trade from ropes and baskets, cork floats hanging on the wall to the left of the door, sou'westers and fishwife's hat.

NEWLYN, FISHERMEN 1906 56532
The donkey and cart, known as a 'Callington' cart, was a typical sight in Newlyn. Used for transporting fish and often the property of 'Jowsters', fish sellers who traveled the district selling fresh fish.

NEWLYN, OLD FISHERWOMAN 1906 56530
These redoubtable women tramped the district selling fish that they carried in a 'cowal' a fish basket whose weight was taken up by a strap that passed round the brow of the fishwife's bonnet. The fishwife in the picture wears a shawl and a 'towser' apron. She carries in her free hand some smoked haddock threaded on to a stick.

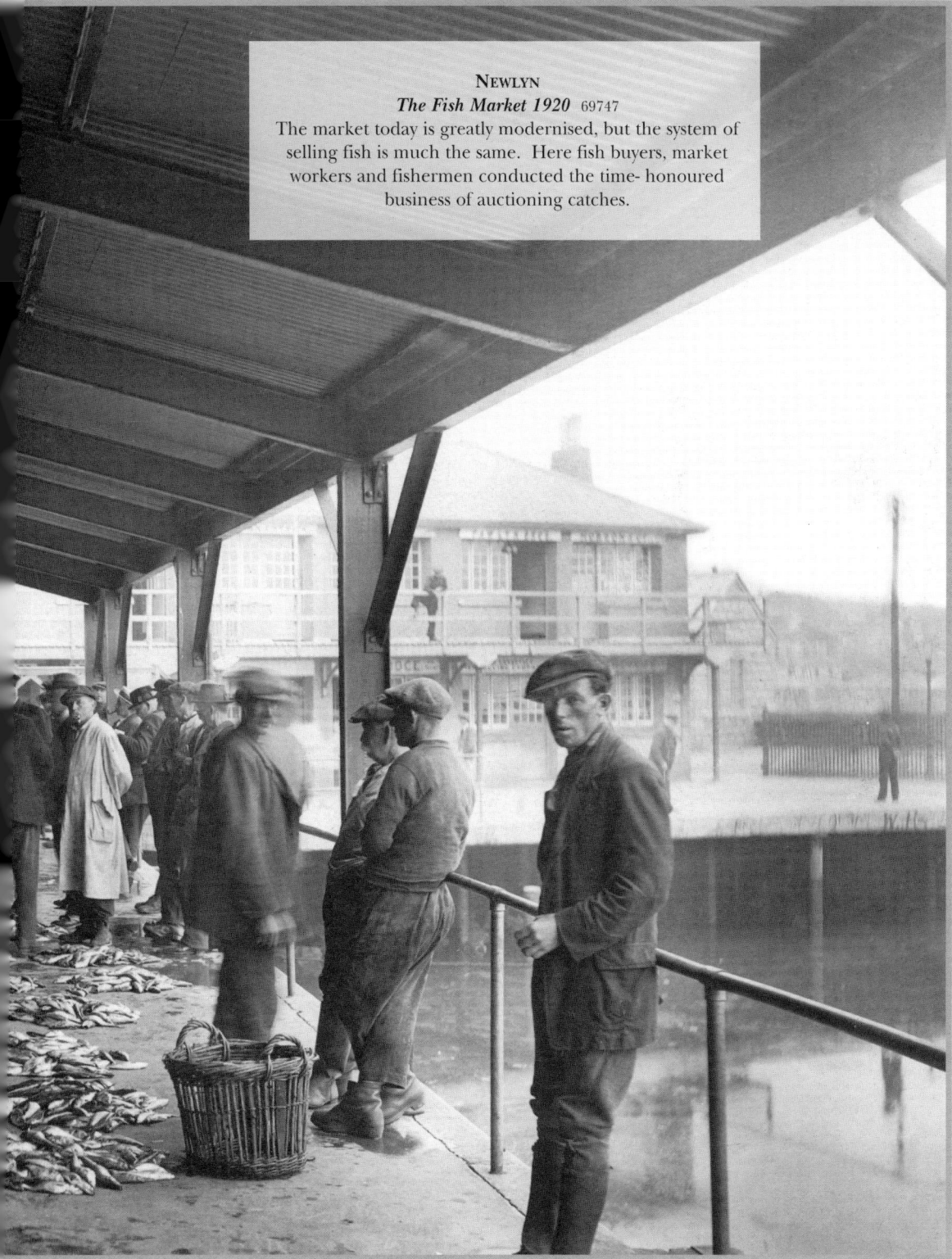

NEWLYN
The Fish Market 1920 69747
The market today is greatly modernised, but the system of selling fish is much the same. Here fish buyers, market workers and fishermen conducted the time- honoured business of auctioning catches.

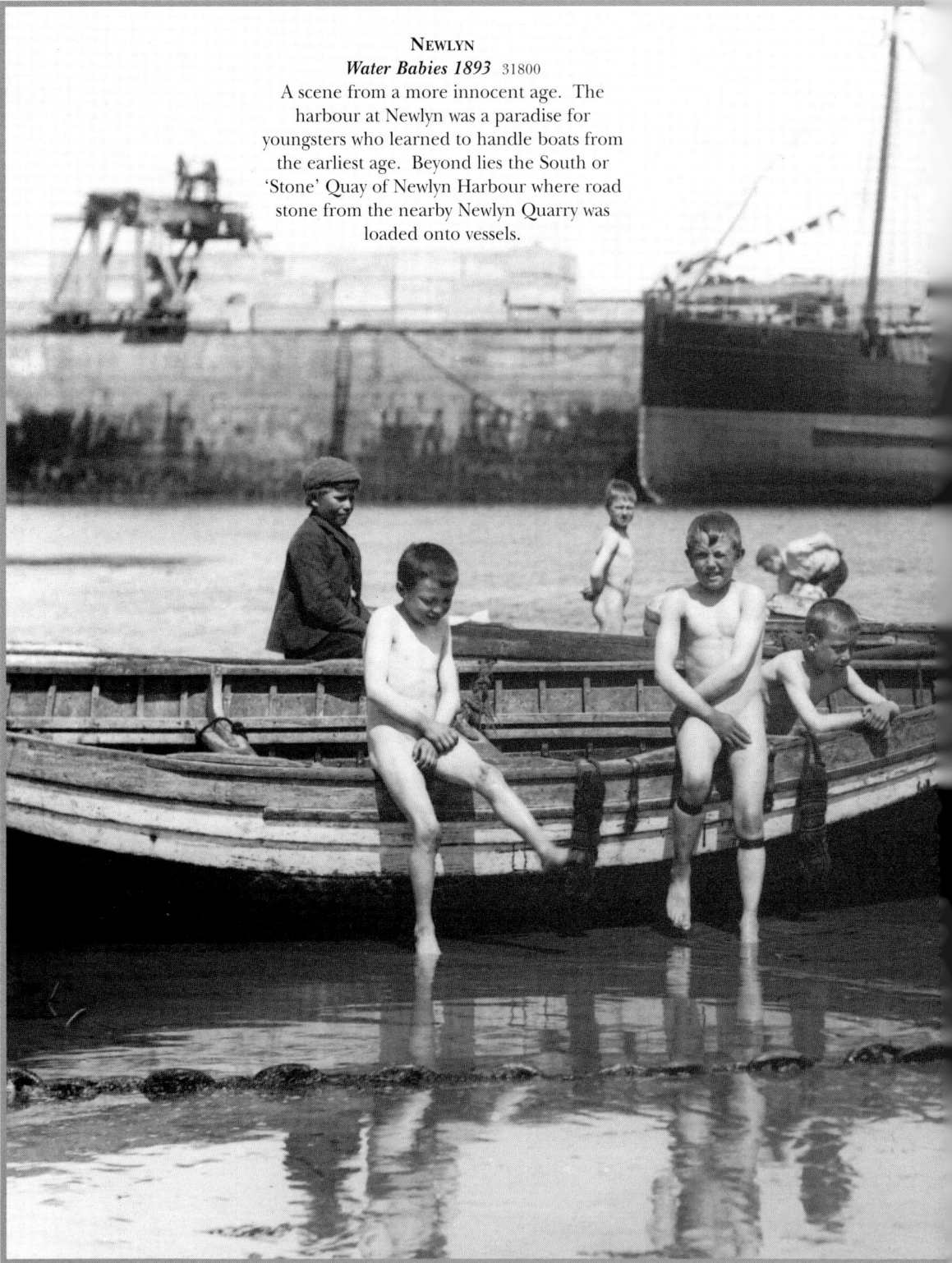

NEWLYN
Water Babies 1893 31800
A scene from a more innocent age. The harbour at Newlyn was a paradise for youngsters who learned to handle boats from the earliest age. Beyond lies the South or 'Stone' Quay of Newlyn Harbour where road stone from the nearby Newlyn Quarry was loaded onto vessels.

PENZANCE, THE BOWLING GREEN c1960 P40119
Bowling is very popular in Penzance, and the town still boasts two greens. This one is situated close to the sea in the popular Bolitho Gardens.

ST MICHAEL'S MOUNT 1908 60982
The Mount can be reached by ferry, or by a stone causeway at low tide. A steep climb leads to the priory church and the superb castle at the top, both of which are open to the public at certain times.

MOUSEHOLE, THE HARBOUR 1927 79945
The village has spread greatly since this time but the picture shows how perfectly Mousehole fits the classic pattern of a Cornish fishing village with the sheltering harbour at its heart and the granite cottages clustered round.

Index

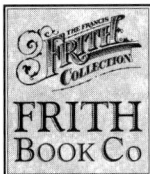

Frith Book Co Titles

www.francisfrith.co.uk

The Frith Book Company publishes over 100 new titles each year. A selection of those currently available are listed below. For latest catalogue please contact Frith Book Co.

Town Books 96 pages, approx 100 photos. County and Themed Books 128 pages, approx 150 photos (unless specified). All titles hardback laminated case and jacket except those indicated pb (paperback)

Amersham, Chesham & Rickmansworth (pb)			Derby (pb)	1-85937-367-4	£9.99
	1-85937-340-2	£9.99	Derbyshire (pb)	1-85937-196-5	£9.99
Ancient Monuments & Stone Circles	1-85937-143-4	£17.99	Devon (pb)	1-85937-297-x	£9.99
Aylesbury (pb)	1-85937-227-9	£9.99	Dorset (pb)	1-85937-269-4	£9.99
Bakewell	1-85937-113-2	£12.99	Dorset Churches	1-85937-172-8	£17.99
Barnstaple (pb)	1-85937-300-3	£9.99	Dorset Coast (pb)	1-85937-299-6	£9.99
Bath (pb)	1-85937419-0	£9.99	Dorset Living Memories	1-85937-210-4	£14.99
Bedford (pb)	1-85937-205-8	£9.99	Down the Severn	1-85937-118-3	£14.99
Berkshire (pb)	1-85937-191-4	£9.99	Down the Thames (pb)	1-85937-278-3	£9.99
Berkshire Churches	1-85937-170-1	£17.99	Down the Trent	1-85937-311-9	£14.99
Blackpool (pb)	1-85937-382-8	£9.99	Dublin (pb)	1-85937-231-7	£9.99
Bognor Regis (pb)	1-85937-431-x	£9.99	East Anglia (pb)	1-85937-265-1	£9.99
Bournemouth	1-85937-067-5	£12.99	East London	1-85937-080-2	£14.99
Bradford (pb)	1-85937-204-x	£9.99	East Sussex	1-85937-130-2	£14.99
Brighton & Hove(pb)	1-85937-192-2	£8.99	Eastbourne	1-85937-061-6	£12.99
Bristol (pb)	1-85937-264-3	£9.99	Edinburgh (pb)	1-85937-193-0	£8.99
British Life A Century Ago (pb)	1-85937-213-9	£9.99	England in the 1880s	1-85937-331-3	£17.99
Buckinghamshire (pb)	1-85937-200-7	£9.99	English Castles (pb)	1-85937-434-4	£9.99
Camberley (pb)	1-85937-222-8	£9.99	English Country Houses	1-85937-161-2	£17.99
Cambridge (pb)	1-85937-422-0	£9.99	Essex (pb)	1-85937-270-8	£9.99
Cambridgeshire (pb)	1-85937-420-4	£9.99	Exeter	1-85937-126-4	£12.99
Canals & Waterways (pb)	1-85937-291-0	£9.99	Exmoor	1-85937-132-9	£14.99
Canterbury Cathedral (pb)	1-85937-179-5	£9.99	Falmouth	1-85937-066-7	£12.99
Cardiff (pb)	1-85937-093-4	£9.99	Folkestone (pb)	1-85937-124-8	£9.99
Carmarthenshire	1-85937-216-3	£14.99	Glasgow (pb)	1-85937-190-6	£9.99
Chelmsford (pb)	1-85937-310-0	£9.99	Gloucestershire	1-85937-102-7	£14.99
Cheltenham (pb)	1-85937-095-0	£9.99	Great Yarmouth (pb)	1-85937-426-3	£9.99
Cheshire (pb)	1-85937-271-6	£9.99	Greater Manchester (pb)	1-85937-266-x	£9.99
Chester	1-85937-090-x	£12.99	Guildford (pb)	1-85937-410-7	£9.99
Chesterfield	1-85937-378-x	£9.99	Hampshire (pb)	1-85937-279-1	£9.99
Chichester (pb)	1-85937-228-7	£9.99	Hampshire Churches (pb)	1-85937-207-4	£9.99
Colchester (pb)	1-85937-188-4	£8.99	Harrogate	1-85937-423-9	£9.99
Cornish Coast	1-85937-163-9	£14.99	Hastings & Bexhill (pb)	1-85937-131-0	£9.99
Cornwall (pb)	1-85937-229-5	£9.99	Heart of Lancashire (pb)	1-85937-197-3	£9.99
Cornwall Living Memories	1-85937-248-1	£14.99	Helston (pb)	1-85937-214-7	£9.99
Cotswolds (pb)	1-85937-230-9	£9.99	Hereford (pb)	1-85937-175-2	£9.99
Cotswolds Living Memories	1-85937-255-4	£14.99	Herefordshire	1-85937-174-4	£14.99
County Durham	1-85937-123-x	£14.99	Hertfordshire (pb)	1-85937-247-3	£9.99
Croydon Living Memories	1-85937-162-0	£9.99	Horsham (pb)	1-85937-432-8	£9.99
Cumbria	1-85937-101-9	£14.99	Humberside	1-85937-215-5	£14.99
Dartmoor	1-85937-145-0	£14.99	Hythe, Romney Marsh & Ashford	1-85937-256-2	£9.99

Available from your local bookshop or from the publisher

Frith Book Co Titles (continued)

Title	ISBN	Price	Title	ISBN	Price
Ipswich (pb)	1-85937-424-7	£9.99	St Ives (pb)	1-85937415-8	£9.99
Ireland (pb)	1-85937-181-7	£9.99	Scotland (pb)	1-85937-182-5	£9.99
Isle of Man (pb)	1-85937-268-6	£9.99	Scottish Castles (pb)	1-85937-323-2	£9.99
Isles of Scilly	1-85937-136-1	£14.99	Sevenoaks & Tunbridge	1-85937-057-8	£12.99
Isle of Wight (pb)	1-85937-429-8	£9.99	Sheffield, South Yorks (pb)	1-85937-267-8	£9.99
Isle of Wight Living Memories	1-85937-304-6	£14.99	Shrewsbury (pb)	1-85937-325-9	£9.99
Kent (pb)	1-85937-189-2	£9.99	Shropshire (pb)	1-85937-326-7	£9.99
Kent Living Memories	1-85937-125-6	£14.99	Somerset	1-85937-153-1	£14.99
Lake District (pb)	1-85937-275-9	£9.99	South Devon Coast	1-85937-107-8	£14.99
Lancaster, Morecambe & Heysham (pb)	1-85937-233-3	£9.99	South Devon Living Memories	1-85937-168-x	£14.99
Leeds (pb)	1-85937-202-3	£9.99	South Hams	1-85937-220-1	£14.99
Leicester	1-85937-073-x	£12.99	Southampton (pb)	1-85937-427-1	£9.99
Leicestershire (pb)	1-85937-185-x	£9.99	Southport (pb)	1-85937-425-5	£9.99
Lincolnshire (pb)	1-85937-433-6	£9.99	Staffordshire	1-85937-047-0	£12.99
Liverpool & Merseyside (pb)	1-85937-234-1	£9.99	Stratford upon Avon	1-85937-098-5	£12.99
London (pb)	1-85937-183-3	£9.99	Suffolk (pb)	1-85937-221-x	£9.99
Ludlow (pb)	1-85937-176-0	£9.99	Suffolk Coast	1-85937-259-7	£14.99
Luton (pb)	1-85937-235-x	£9.99	Surrey (pb)	1-85937-240-6	£9.99
Maidstone	1-85937-056-x	£14.99	Sussex (pb)	1-85937-184-1	£9.99
Manchester (pb)	1-85937-198-1	£9.99	Swansea (pb)	1-85937-167-1	£9.99
Middlesex	1-85937-158-2	£14.99	Tees Valley & Cleveland	1-85937-211-2	£14.99
New Forest	1-85937-128-0	£14.99	Thanet (pb)	1-85937-116-7	£9.99
Newark (pb)	1-85937-366-6	£9.99	Tiverton (pb)	1-85937-178-7	£9.99
Newport, Wales (pb)	1-85937-258-9	£9.99	Torbay	1-85937-063-2	£12.99
Newquay (pb)	1-85937-421-2	£9.99	Truro	1-85937-147-7	£12.99
Norfolk (pb)	1-85937-195-7	£9.99	Victorian and Edwardian Cornwall	1-85937-252-x	£14.99
Norfolk Living Memories	1-85937-217-1	£14.99	Victorian & Edwardian Devon	1-85937-253-8	£14.99
Northamptonshire	1-85937-150-7	£14.99	Victorian & Edwardian Kent	1-85937-149-3	£14.99
Northumberland Tyne & Wear (pb)	1-85937-281-3	£9.99	Vic & Ed Maritime Album	1-85937-144-2	£17.99
North Devon Coast	1-85937-146-9	£14.99	Victorian and Edwardian Sussex	1-85937-157-4	£14.99
North Devon Living Memories	1-85937-261-9	£14.99	Victorian & Edwardian Yorkshire	1-85937-154-x	£14.99
North London	1-85937-206-6	£14.99	Victorian Seaside	1-85937-159-0	£17.99
North Wales (pb)	1-85937-298-8	£9.99	Villages of Devon (pb)	1-85937-293-7	£9.99
North Yorkshire (pb)	1-85937-236-8	£9.99	Villages of Kent (pb)	1-85937-294-5	£9.99
Norwich (pb)	1-85937-194-9	£8.99	Villages of Sussex (pb)	1-85937-295-3	£9.99
Nottingham (pb)	1-85937-324-0	£9.99	Warwickshire (pb)	1-85937-203-1	£9.99
Nottinghamshire (pb)	1-85937-187-6	£9.99	Welsh Castles (pb)	1-85937-322-4	£9.99
Oxford (pb)	1-85937-411-5	£9.99	West Midlands (pb)	1-85937-289-9	£9.99
Oxfordshire (pb)	1-85937-430-1	£9.99	West Sussex	1-85937-148-5	£14.99
Peak District (pb)	1-85937-280-5	£9.99	West Yorkshire (pb)	1-85937-201-5	£9.99
Penzance	1-85937-069-1	£12.99	Weymouth (pb)	1-85937-209-0	£9.99
Peterborough (pb)	1-85937-219-8	£9.99	Wiltshire (pb)	1-85937-277-5	£9.99
Piers	1-85937-237-6	£17.99	Wiltshire Churches (pb)	1-85937-171-x	£9.99
Plymouth	1-85937-119-1	£12.99	Wiltshire Living Memories	1-85937-245-7	£14.99
Poole & Sandbanks (pb)	1-85937-251-1	£9.99	Winchester (pb)	1-85937-428-x	£9.99
Preston (pb)	1-85937-212-0	£9.99	Windmills & Watermills	1-85937-242-2	£17.99
Reading (pb)	1-85937-238-4	£9.99	Worcester (pb)	1-85937-165-5	£9.99
Romford (pb)	1-85937-319-4	£9.99	Worcestershire	1-85937-152-3	£14.99
Salisbury (pb)	1-85937-239-2	£9.99	York (pb)	1-85937-199-x	£9.99
Scarborough (pb)	1-85937-379-8	£9.99	Yorkshire (pb)	1-85937-186-8	£9.99
St Albans (pb)	1-85937-341-0	£9.99	Yorkshire Living Memories	1-85937-166-3	£14.99

See Frith books on the internet www.francisfrith.co.uk

Frith Products & Services

Francis Frith would doubtless be pleased to know that the pioneering publishing venture he started in 1860 still continues today. A hundred and forty years later, The Francis Frith Collection continues in the same innovative tradition and is now one of the foremost publishers of vintage photographs in the world. Some of the current activities include:

Interior Decoration

Today Frith's photographs can be seen framed and as giant wall murals in thousands of pubs, restaurants, hotels, banks, retail stores and other public buildings throughout the country. In every case they enhance the unique local atmosphere of the places they depict and provide reminders of gentler days in an increasingly busy and frenetic world.

Product Promotions

Frith products are used by many major companies to promote the sales of their own products or to reinforce their own history and heritage. Frith promotions have been used by Hovis bread, Courage beers, Scots Porage Oats, Colman's mustard, Cadbury's foods, Mellow Birds coffee, Dunhill pipe tobacco, Guinness, and Bulmer's Cider.

Genealogy and Family History

As the interest in family history and roots grows world-wide, more and more people are turning to Frith's photographs of Great Britain for images of the towns, villages and streets where their ancestors lived; and, of course, photographs of the churches and chapels where their ancestors were christened, married and buried are an essential part of every genealogy tree and family album.

Frith Products

All Frith photographs are available Framed or just as Mounted Prints and Posters (size 23 x 16 inches). These may be ordered from the address below. From time to time other products - Address Books, Calendars, Table Mats, etc - are available.

The Internet

Already twenty thousand Frith photographs can be viewed and purchased on the internet through the Frith websites and a myriad of partner sites.

For more detailed information on Frith companies and products, look at these sites:

www.francisfrith.co.uk
www.francisfrith.com
(for North American visitors)

See the complete list of Frith Books at:

www.francisfrith.co.uk

This web site is regularly updated with the latest list of publications from the Frith Book Company. If you wish to buy books relating to another part of the country that your local bookshop does not stock, you may purchase on-line.

For further information, trade, or author enquiries please contact us at the address below:
The Francis Frith Collection, Frith's Barn, Teffont, Salisbury, Wiltshire, England SP3 5QP.
Tel: +44 (0)1722 716 376 Fax: +44 (0)1722 716 881 Email: sales@francisfrith.co.uk

See Frith books on the internet www.francisfrith.co.uk

TO RECEIVE YOUR **FREE** MOUNTED PRINT

Mounted Print
Overall size 14 x 11 inches

Cut out this Voucher and return it with your remittance for £1.95 to cover postage and handling, to UK addresses. For overseas addresses please include £4.00 post and handling. Choose any photograph included in this book. Your SEPIA print will be A4 in size, and mounted in a cream mount with burgundy rule line, overall size 14 x 11 inches.

Order additional Mounted Prints at HALF PRICE (only £7.49 each*)

If there are further pictures you would like to order, possibly as gifts for friends and family, purchase them at half price (no additional postage and handling required).

Have your Mounted Prints framed*

For an additional £14.95 per print you can have your chosen Mounted Print framed in an elegant polished wood and gilt moulding, overall size 16 x 13 inches (no additional postage and handling required).

---

* IMPORTANT!
These special prices are only available if ordered using the original voucher on this page (no copies permitted) and at the same time as your free Mounted Print, for delivery to the same address

---

Frith Collectors' Guild

From time to time we publish a magazine of news and stories about Frith photographs and further special offers of Frith products. If you would like 12 months FREE membership, please return this form.

Send completed forms to:
The Francis Frith Collection, Frith's Barn, Teffont, Salisbury, Wiltshire SP3 5QP

Voucher for **FREE** and Reduced Price Frith Prints

Picture no.	Page number	Qty	Mounted @ £7.49	Framed + £14.95	Total Cost
		1	**Free of charge***	£	£
			£7.49	£	£
			£7.49	£	£
			£7.49	£	£
			£7.49	£	£
			£7.49	£	£

Please allow 28 days for delivery   *** Post & handling**   **£1.95**

Book Title . . . .   **Total Order Cost**   £

Please do not photocopy this voucher. Only the original is valid, so please cut it out and return it to us.

I enclose a cheque / postal order for £ . . . .
made payable to 'The Francis Frith Collection'
OR please debit my Mastercard / Visa / Switch / Amex card
(credit cards please on all overseas orders)

Number . . . .

Issue No(Switch only) . . . . .Valid from (Amex/Switch) . . . .

Expires . . . . Signature . . . .

Name Mr/Mrs/Ms . . . .

Address . . . .

. . . .

. . . . Postcode . . . .

Daytime Tel No . . . .   Valid to 31/12/03

The Francis Frith Collectors' Guild

Please enrol me as a member for 12 months free of charge.

Name Mr/Mrs/Ms . . . .

Address . . . .

. . . .

. . . . Postcode . . . .

Would you like to find out more about Francis Frith?

We have recently recruited some entertaining speakers who are happy to visit local groups, clubs and societies to give an illustrated talk documenting Frith's travels and photographs. If you are a member of such a group and are interested in hosting a presentation, we would love to hear from you.

Our speakers bring with them a small selection of our local town and county books, together with sample prints. They are happy to take orders. A small proportion of the order value is donated to the group who have hosted the presentation. The talks are therefore an excellent way of fundraising for small groups and societies.

Can you help us with information about any of the Frith photographs in this book?

We are gradually compiling an historical record for each of the photographs in the Frith archive. It is always fascinating to find out the names of the people shown in the pictures, as well as insights into the shops, buildings and other features depicted.

If you recognize anyone in the photographs in this book, or if you have information not already included in the author's caption, do let us know. We would love to hear from you, and will try to publish it in future books or articles.

Our production team

Frith books are produced by a small dedicated team at offices in the converted Grade II listed 18th-century barn at Teffont near Salisbury, illustrated above. Most have worked with the Frith Collection for many years. All have in common one quality: they have a passion for the Frith Collection. The team is constantly expanding, but currently includes:

Jason Buck, John Buck, Douglas Burns, Heather Crisp, Lucy Elcock, Isobel Hall, Rob Hames, Hazel Heaton, Peter Horne, James Kinnear, Tina Leary, Hannah Marsh, Eliza Sackett, Terence Sackett, Sandra Sanger, Lewis Taylor, Shelley Tolcher, Helen Vimpany, Clive Wathen and Jenny Wathen.

Free Print - see overleaf